ME...
WORDS

CASSIUS D. MCPHERSON

Halo ●●●●
Publishing International

ISBN: 978-1-61244-494-9
Library of Congress Control Number: 2016911837

Printed in the United States of America

Halo ●●●●
Publishing International
www.halopublishing.com

Published by Halo Publishing International
1100 NW Loop 410
Suite 700 - 176
San Antonio, Texas 78213
Toll Free 1-877-705-9647
Website: www.halopublishing.com
E-mail: contact@halopublishing.com

I dedicate this book to the world; we as people have forgotten the true concept of LIFE! We kill without remorse life today seems to have no value.

To my wife Linda A (Marsh) McPherson, I love you now as I did the day we married you are by far one of the strongest women I have ever met, just knowing you made me a stronger person, you will always be the one to inspire my writings. My two boys Byron Nelson, Kevin Robinson gone from us to soon you will always be in my heart. As always my mother and my sister Willie C McPherson & Annette McPherson I miss you ladies so much but your always with me...ALWAYS

THIS GENERATION! You are the future, things are moving and growing so fast, slow down live life don't let life live you.

Thanks Cassius

Contents

IN HIS FIRST BOOK "THOUGHTS FROM AN ADDICTED MIND," CASSIUS SHARED HIS JOURNEY BACK INTO CIVILIAN LIVING. AFTER BEING INJURED IN IRAQ AND FINDIND HIMSELF BATTLING DRUGS AND P.T.S.D.

HE IS NOW SHOWING HIS GROWTH THROUGH MERE WORDS. CASSIUS HAS SHOWN THAT WORDS CAN AND WILL HEAL. ENJOY HIS LATEST JOURNEY AS HE CONTINUES TO GROW WITH THE USE OF MERE WORDS.

THANK-YOU

As I watched with millions the swearing in of our First Black President.

I couldn't help but think of those pioneers who missed this Historic event.

They paved the way for greatness they suffered so we could be free.

To see a Black Man finally taking the oath for Office of Presidency.

But let us not forget the fight, the lives lost for us to be.

Here today! because what we call struggling our ancestors called being free.

Look deep into the eyes of our elders in their eyes you'll see relief.

Were here because of our Ancestors to see a Black Commander in Chief.

So thank-you to those who survived the slave ships, beatings and disrespect.

The back of the bus the white on black lust, the noose around your neck.

They fought for our civil rights a fight still fought today.

An historical day for the country, still for our ancestors I pray.

I pray that they see closure that we've finished what they begun.

Were here because they endured captivity being raped, tortured and hung.

Today I'm proud to be in the skin I'm in, I was here when HIS- STORY was made.

Today maybe some of those memories of slavery will now began to fade. Still the dream is our Ancestors Legacy for them I celebrate. The lives that was given in the name of freedom is what makes this day so great. So thank-you to all the pioneers who endured all the pain and drama. For us to be here and be able to cheer for

"PRESIDENT BARACK OBAMA"

DELETE

Corruption in our government our economy isn't right.

See green is the only color that matters there is no black or white.

Our votes are supposed to make a change yet again we face defeat.

But I believe there's a way to ease the pain, with a plan I call delete.

The student loans and back taxes they know will not be paid.

If delete had been pushed by G.W Bush, we may forget the mistakes he made.

We Have families struggling to feed their kids, can barely make ends meet.

See the deficit would simply disappear if they would only press delete.

We destroyed IRAQI with Bush's war now we're paying for the reconstruction.

A lie to deprive them of their oil called weapons of mass-destruction.

Gas prices are dropping; let's see how long this drop will last.

Before they come up with another method to stick taxes up our ass.

We'll here we're doing all we can, they'll try to be discrete.

But there's only one way to make it all go away Delete! Delete! Delete!

My prayers will be with our president as He face's what lies ahead.

Because the Dream has become a nightmare and the economies stuck in RED.

From Him I don't expect a miracle any change would beat defeat.

if I was OBAMA I'd bypass the drama and simply press DELETE.

I can't understand the master plan behind sending out stimulus checks.

Still the deficit remains so how the hell do we gain is this not politically incorrect.

So given this plan I offer you and seeing an economy bound for defeat.

See the proof in the plan point your finger lift your hand and press DELETE! DELETE! DELETE!

IN THE COVER OF NIGHT

Morning seems to never come the darkness never ends.

The streets are filled with madness Lord forgive us for our sins.

A crying child in the cover of night endless cries of hurt.

An endless trail of terror expressed on a bloody shirt.

Drug infested children a generation bound to burn.

We blame it on teachers, put too much trust in preachers, there's a lesson to be learned.

Dark images appear in your mind; you find yourself deeply sighing.

Your emotions are at a crossroads, it's your soul that's gently crying.

Your thoughts elude your being as you attempt to win the fight.

Yet the rain can't hide your teardrops in the cover of the night.

Mere wonderous thoughts of nothingness as we stare deeply into space.

Time flies by no matter how hard we try; we'll never win this race.

Somewhere in these words is a message in the darkness these words are right.

But the lights were dim when I wrote this poem in the cover of the night.

"STRESS"

An emotional killer the devils ace in the hole.

The only thing that's capable of damaging your soul.

It creeps into your life as quite as a breeze.

Corrupting all things around you, never aims to please.

It enters lives through choices, made by you or someone close.

Destroying love and lives but it's your heart that hurts the most.

"STRESS"

An emotional killer the devils ace in the hole.

The only thing that's capable of damaging your soul.

A constant pain inside you, your pressures on the boil.

Whatever happiness your searching for "STRESS" is going to foil.

Its "STRESS" the devil's playbook and he's running it like a pro.

You must have a plan to counter his play or into the hole you go.

"STRESS"

An emotional killer the devils ace in the hole.

The only thing that's capable of damaging your soul

It lurks within our memories appears inside our dreams.

Rips through the fabrics of our lives tears us at the seams.

We hold this hurt inside us until its way to late.

Now it's not a battle its now a great debate.

"WITH STRESS"

BELEIFS CHURCHES AND TITHES

My faith in the Lord is real, I believe Jesus Christ died for my sins.

I thank the Lord every morning my feet touch the floor.

I don't just pray when times get hard or when there is wrong in my life. I understand that He is the beginning and the end of what we so freely call "LIFE." I openly confess my love for the Lord, I respect church but don't go often. But when I do I praise just as hard as an avid goer.

I also believe that tithes are more than just money, GOD said give of your wealth. Some of us just aren't wealthy enough to give money. If you share time with someone who is less fortunate then you That's a Tithe. If you take the time to pray for someone other than yourself, That's a Tithe.

Anything that can brighten and or enlighten the life of another this I believe in the eyes of the LORD is a Tithe.

So my question is if I drink does this make me a non-believer?

If I sometimes use bad language in anger does that make me less a believer?

If I don't go to church every Sunday and give monetary tithes does that make me less a believer?

I believe it's wrong to judge anyone regardless of their life style,

None of us are perfect.

We all have flaws and problems; all he truly asks is we believe in him If that is truly in your heart. Is to believe more important than church? Is appearance and monetary tithes one give judge worthy?

One should not be judged by man or women by belief or lifestyle that job is already taken.

"RELENTLESS"

I have withstood the pains of hard times.

Yet I still sit in awe at life.

Countless mistakes made over a span of constant

moments that reflect cold memories of what we call life.

Now standing in the middle of your emotional

stalemate, you glance mercifully in a direction which

at that moment you sit in awe at what we call life.

"RELENTLESS"

When you find yourself wondering about nothing.

That inner peace where time seems to pause,

you reflect on images not stories images past

trophies. Your empty thoughts endless

nothings, again you sit is awe at what we call

LIFE.

"RELENTLESS"

Now imagine being sold like a pair of jeans.

Being bunched up like a strawberry in a basket.

Being shot in groups by a firing squad.

Being hung by your neck for doing something

Stupid, spending your life behind bars.

When you truly think of their suffering at

that moment aren't we?

"RELENTLESS"

LOSING SITE.

Darkness has engulfed us it's hard to see the light.

We're losing site of what's important, what is wrong or right.

Babies having baby's parents doing dope.

Families being torn apart there seems to be no hope.

Will history repeat itself will we ever see the light.

Will we forever walk in darkness; I fear were losing site.

Of really what's important how hard can this really be.

We're losing site of our children's dreams losing site of reality.

We're fighting wars in other countries, still we Have wars right here at home.

Drugs murder gangs and guns life in a thunder dome.

Children born with drugs in their systems parents locked away.

Mothers selling their bodies for drugs father run away.

It's cold and lonely in this world and I fear were losing the fight.

We're giving up on our children I'm afraid we're losing site.

THE BLAME

We blame it on alcohol and drugs. We blame it on the streets.

We blame it on politicians yet we voted to fill those seats.

We blame it on the parents. We blame it on the schools.

We place blame where blame shouldn't be now that's a chain for fools.

We blame it on tv hell we blame it on games and rap.

But I've never seen one of these entities equal dirt nap.

We try to find a scape goat to blame for our mistakes.

All of which is irrelevant to the choices that we make.

Our children are committing crimes that we never thought of doing.

We blame the streets and drug dealers for the life that their pursuing.

Now let's be quaint about this we can go over this again and again.

We failed and now we're failing them we truly are the BLAME.

THE STRUGGLE

It haunts us through our memories, it's still alive today.

As long as racism is taught it will never go away.

The struggle to live as an equal, just be treated the same.

To not be called a Nigger or let the noose re-enters the game.

They can't rewrite our history our ancestors saw to that.

But a racist will never let this disease become an artifact.

Malcom and Martin didn't wait for a reason to fight the fight.

They died for the struggle for us to be free, we're the ones losing site.

We don't need more black politicians, King never campaigned for votes.

We need more black teachers and leaders to create more antidotes.

A great man said it in three words for new leadership we yearn.

Our ancestors died for the struggle three words "ITS YOUR TURN".

BROKEN DREAMS

So often I fight within myself, I'm losing so it seems.

I fight to find an answer to fix my broken dreams.

Uncontrollable thoughts invade the portals of my mind.

I can't control these feelings where do I draw the line.

Broken dreams are promises to ourselves we made.

In reality our broken dreams are memories that fade.

I fight with my emotions I yearn to find the truth.

My broken dreams are nightmares that haunts me from my youth.

I've opened up Pandora's box and can't seem to close it back.

My life is like an open book I'm falling through the cracks.

I reach up toward the heavens to suppress my broken dreams.

I can't unlock this closet; no one hears my screams.

I stare in awe at my memories still its tearing me at the seams.

I fight to find some inner peace inside my broken dreams.

NOOSE

Never overlook our slavery evolvement

Our ancestors evolved from slavery and our evolvement continues today.

If we forget from which we come from racism will never go away.

A legacy of fighters fought and died for us to be free.

We're letting a rope tied in the form of a noose take up space in our reality.

Ignorance is racist a vicious cycle this may be.

But I won't allow this cycle to take the dream away from me.

A noose always a PAINFUL site still with numbers we prevail.

Our ancestors were tried by the noose their blood is our holy grail.

Never overlook our slavery evolvement for new leaders do we yearn.

A new generation of fighters I do believe it's now your turn.

To take the torch our ancestors lit and proudly carry-on.

The fight our ancestors died for a new story to be born.

Never overlook our slavery evolvement a new hatred is on the loose.

Their reminding us it's alive in the hearts of many in the form of a hangman's NOOSE...

I REMEMBER

I remember watching my elders laugh drink and have fun.

I remember watching my elders play and joke with loaded guns.

I remember watching them watching me as they played spades and bid wiz.

I remember as a child saying to myself, I cant wait till I can do this.

I remember being hungry cause we had no food to eat.

I remember my socks being soaked, because I had holes in the shoes on my feet.

I remember seeing my mother cry, wondering what was wrong.

I remember her turning to dry those tears to show me she was strong.

I remember when neighbors were concerned about the blocks.

I remember sitting out late at night, no one was slanging rocks.

I remember building Go karts, playing in the park.

I remember when parents felt safe enough to let their kids stay out till dark.

Now I'm 53yrs old and these memories are very, very clear.

I've sat and cried because I hurt inside, see our children live in fear.

If I can remember theses 53yrs from January to December. Imagine what they see and what their children are going to remember.

SILENT TEARS

They mimic everything they see as they learn throughout the years.

Painful memories off abuse expressed through silent tears.

Depressed memories in the head of a child anger lie in wait.

They can't understand being slapped by the hand that told you not to hate.

Being raised in a home that has no love with no reason to laugh or cheer.

A child unable to show love or affection drowning in silent tears.

They can't concentrate on school work the home is filled with grief.

So they take to gangbangers and drug dealers in search for some relief.

Young minds filled with failure how could they understand.

Seeing mommy sell her body everyday a different man.

Theses' children are crying out for help still they hide their deepest fears.

Holding them in then the cycle begins in the form of silent tears.

A wall of loneliness engulfs them as they deal with life on life terms.

Then they bury themselves in a make believe grave only missing the worms.

Still they soak up information in the form of blunts and beers.

Then when their grown with kids of their own they too will face silent tears.

THE PAVEMENT

Sand rocks and water the mixture for quick cement.

Too often a final resting place face down on the pavement.

The death toll is on the rise from city to city, someday we may see.

Crime become a subject in schools called Black History.

The streets are educating our children to be dealers thugs and pimps.

They make the generation before them look like clergymen mascots and wimps.

The pavement is a battle ground, its ran with an iron fist.

We're losing our children to the pavement, their disappearing in the mist.

Some of our so called leaders stand quietly in the back.

Then as soon as a child is unjustly accused they remember that their black.

We have homeless Veterans pounding the pavement in search of a place to sleep.

Still the government is spending BILLIONS on war, the research for cloning sheep.

We're losing our children to the pavement, they'll lose their children too.

The Pavement is unforgiving when the outline on the ground is you.

WHAT IS LIFE

The question without an answer the question what is life?

Each day is a circle of past dreams or thoughts sinking into a cavern of nightmares.

Yet the question remains what is life?

I've asked myself this question and as hard as it may seem.

Life is just a moment based on past nightmares and dreams.

Collective thoughts of nothingness all wrapped up in one.

What is life Is the question? answers I have none.

A common goal to some it seems to others an unreachable dream.

A room filled with doors and invisible floors nightly they scream.

I lift my head above the clouds to ask the father why?

My pain rains down in buckets I've made the father cry.

I can't explain day today it cuts me like a knife.

The question remains without an answer the question is what is life?

INNER MOST

Dwelling deep within ones being a scrambled group of dreams.

The echoes of silence invade your soul yet you hear the screams.

You search for a piece of solace or a peaceful place to run.

But darkness has engulfed you you're now a loaded gun.

Your reaching for emotional straws trying to make since of it all.

Still every time you reach the top of one hill the further you seem to fall.

Your loathing in self-pity drowning in a sea of guilt.

You're like a rose out of water bout to dry and wilt.

Your running in the same spot your shoes now have no sole.

Your empty like time and space lifeless no soul.

Stuck like a deer in headlights stunned without a clue.

It's those inner most thoughts fighting inside trying to get out of you.

Inner most thoughts rambling dreams stuck inside your head.

Erase the madness maintain control or you just might wind up dead.

SO

So you finally opened up your mind to face reality?

So the life that you decided to pursue is not what you thought it would be?

So you sit and wonder what to do still your mind is running blank?

So you ask yourself who's to blame, you're the one you have to thank?

So you give life a thought about the happiness you sought as the tears flow thru the night?

So now you shake of the cobwebs of life in search of a place to run?

So much pressure to change your life feels deranged, your emotionally beaten and stunned.

So as darkness clouds your chain of thought your mind can't comprehend.

So again you sigh to the heavens you cry, please forgive me for my sins.

So you cover your eyes from the answers. So your hidden from the truth?

So you're afraid to concede on the cross did He bleed it's not like pulling a tooth.

So you center yourself like an image unfocused a blur of light?

So still to the eye you see black worms fly still the room is as dark as night.

So many choices how do one choose from this high? I've created a low.

So deep to the mind I'm confused there's a sign as it reads so slowly SO.

FATHER

We call GOD our father, so with the shoes you have to fill.

Your family foundation bring gratification your king of the hill.

A guardian in the time of darkness, a leader to the light.

A decision maker in time of crisis the decider of wrong and right.

The leader of all children be it Boy or Girl.

The overseer of community's protector of the world.

Your task is never easy your load is never light.

Turning boys to men in this chaotic world is an ever ending fight.

Still you've stood through all adversity even when all else fail it seems.

You remembered the fight of our ancestors and held on to the dream.

FATHER! sad that there are some who can't comprehend the responsibility that comes with the title FATHER.

So I'll take this time to give a reminder.

FATHER THE CREATOR OF THE HEAVENS AND EARTH.

LOADED QUESTIONS

You keep on asking questions you already know the answer too.

Then when I tell you it's loaded you claim I'm ignoring you.

Your timings not always perfect my answers not always true.

But your loaded questions are like an unwanted guess only passing through.

No matter what answer I give you the question still the same.

Trying to make a zebra change his stripes is this some kind of game.

Your acting like a high price shrink, I'm always on your couch.

I be waiting to see when you stop grilling me, the pipe comes out the pouch.

You treat me like an insurgent stuck on Guantanamo bay.

Your loaded questions are torturing no matter what I say.

So many times I wondered what will come out your mouth today.

Then you hit me with a loaded question you won't just go away.

See you taught me how to deal with this I pray I've learned my lesson.

Look out for the signs read between the lines and beware the loaded question.

TIME AND SPACE

As I cover these pages with thoughts from my heart my admiration for you grew.

Still this distance lays heavy on my mind my soul is missing you.

A song plays softly in my head the tone is all so clear.

The lyrics begin with I love you, ends with I need you here.

I want for you when I'm awake, I'm with you in my dreams.

I kiss your lips and instantly I'm with you so it seems.

I close my eyes when I'm lonely, you appear and bring me peace.

The loneliness would disappear the pains, I had would cease.

Tormented by my past mistakes that haunts me every night.

I asked Him for your forgiveness as I hold my pillow tight.

I'm longing for the opportunity to roll over, see your face.

I wish to grow old with you holding my soul, filling this time and space.

You give me reason to rise in the morning, a reason to lie at night.

Your love could make the cripple walk, give a blind man sight.

I'll end this with you knowing you place a smile upon my face.

You are the owner of this heart you fill my time and space.

AS IF TIME STOOD STILL

I was mesmerized by your beauty down my spine you sent a chill.

Your as lovely as the first day we met as if time stood still.

Your face is like a work of art GOD surely broke the mold.

You're like a treasure at the end of a rainbow my Queen laced in gold.

I shiver at the mere thought of you please let this love be real.

I'm captured in your loveliness as if time stood still.

As I gazed into your big brown eyes I fell deeper in love with you.

Good women are hard to come by you amongst the chosen few.

As my past stares me in my face it gives me such thrill.

I see you now as I saw you then as if time stood still.

My memories are dreams from my past my past is dreams of you.

My world revolves around your love and everything you do.

So say you'll always love me ant that you all ways will.

Be my past my present my future as if time stood still.

AN ODE TO STEROIDS

Oh multi-million-dollar contract fans in million dollar seats.

The pressure on athletes to perform these days has become an impossible feat.

The way organizations are paying athletes and expecting them to perform.

Taking steroids to enhance your performance in sports has become the norm.

If you don't think kids are taking steroids in school to make the team.

Then ask yourself for a million-dollar contract would you to reach your dreams?

Has the caliber of players changed, haven't a lot of stats went down?

Or has the game became a little more even since steroids aren't around.

We knew this stuff was out there still we watched them do inhuman things.

Hitting 70 homeruns out running bullets from a gun, flying like you got wings.

Do they check for steroids in boxing, hockey hell bowling any less?

Because steroids are in most of the drugs found in our medicine chest.

Scientist have been studying the effects of steroids since laboratories were built.

But the only thing they told the public is you get big and your testicles wilt.

Is it fair that athletes do steroids NO, but are we willing ourselves to admit, that we have no reason to be mad as fans for the part we played in it?

We pay for those high priced tickets to see the players play.

Then when you hear about steroids you have something to say.

We want to start complaining, screaming out words like cheat.

But you're not the one out there playing the game in the rain, cold and heat.

So why do you think they do it, put their bodies through so much shit?

Like Elliot Davis from channel 2 says because you paid for it.

So let the media keep asking rhetorical questions making athletes look dumb and funny.

Until they stop giving meaningless excuses, admit I did it for the money.

THE METHOD TO MY MADDNESS

I've learned to control the environment that raised me.

The method in my madness became the man you now see.

A homeless drug addict that found the will to live.

In the words that came from the darkness, this gift I wish to give.

To the addict searching or comfort an end to all the sadness.

Read well these words I share; you'll see the method in my madness.

Rehabs are just a stepping stone a tool for the average fiend.

See the drugs may be out but without a doubt your mind is still not clean.

We learn thru time to self-medicate and it becomes hard to let it go.

We become depended on drugs to ease the pain its then called old need Moe.

As we hide in our drug addiction reality seems to stall.

The longer we choose to ignore the pain the further we seem to fall.

If you can believe that an addiction is 90% mental and 10% stupidity, then your well on your way.

The method to my madness is the reason I'm here today.

All that pain that grows inside you brought on by drugs and booze.

Your strongest tool to recovery you only have to choose.

You've been hurting inside for far too long it's time to release the pain.

Drugs have controlled your life to long it's time to live again.

ENOUGH

I need you to complete me please hear the word I say.

I declare my love undyingly for you on valentine's day.

My heart exploded with ecstasy my love for you is true.

I can't say enough about our love every minute I'm missing you.

When you're not with me I close my eyes and suddenly you appear.

Then this calmness seems to come over me I need to have you here.

To tell me everything's ok even though time are ruff.

I have nothing to fear for having you here for me is more than enough.

IF I COULD

If I could sprinkle your life with nothing but love and make your worries, go away.

If I could hold you when you cold would surely make my day.

If I could answer all your questions and leave not one stone unturned.

If I could I'd prove my love is real that you're the one, I yearn.

If I could look into your eyes and prove the way I feel.

I promise to stop saying IF I COULD and promise to say I WILL!

IN THE WAKE OF IT ALL

Never really noticing the stillness of the trees.

As the leaves remain restless I still can feel the breeze.

Combined with the horrific trails of life I have managed to stay afloat in the wake of it all.

I paint a picture of life but the colors all run.

I've searched for an artist to complete this piece and found that there is none.

I've oppressed the things in my life that makes no sense a chain reaction now begins a metamorphose will commence.

A drastic change is coming like spring evolves to fall

I've stood strong through all adversities in the wake of it all.

I mask my fears with a blank face in the world I stand alone.

In the wake of it all does anyone have the balls to venture into the unknown.

I cloak my pains from others cause its pain that strengthens me.

I can't explain the logic but its wit me constantly.

I've acknowledged my down falls yet as I fall down in the wake of it all I have survived.

My crossroads has intersected into a highway of lost thoughts.

Still I have been diligent as my roads crossed I stepped back to see what is in store in the wake of it all.

PICTURES

The mind is like a photo album each picture tells a tale.

We focus on them good or bad in our minds they dwell.

We often hold these memories to remind us of the past.

Some are too graphic to surface so a shadow they now cast.

We linger in this photo album searching for the past-tense.

But like dirty laundry in a washing machine it'll all come out in the rinse.

But these pictures can be baffling, in time can cause one grief.

The pain can be unbearable like a dentist pulling teeth.

Life is like a side show that only you can see.

These pictures are stains of past pains stored in your memory.

Now convinced you can control the movie is these pictures seem to be.

The source of all that ails you, the root to your misery.

Repressive are these pictures yet we hold on to them still.

Pictures, photos, memories, expression of how we feel.

MY FEET TOUCH THE FLO.

I acknowledge the fact that He is real every morning when I awake.

He has granted me another day doesn't matter which road I take.

My eyes to see, my ears to hear, a chance for me to grow.

I thank you Lord each morning you allow my feet to touch the flo.

I give thanks every night I raise them, when you lay me down to sleep.

When I'm down your watching over me were demons fear to creep.

I write these words of acknowledged for those who need to know.

My thanks to Him begins the moment my feet touch the flo.

I can't reverse my yesterday so I try to plan ahead.

Still I can't control those hours I lay quietly in my bed.

Tomorrow is not promised so give praise when yours begin.

Understand it's not your choice to choose when your time will end.

Life is His Investment He is the C.E.O.

Acknowledge the fact that He is real soon as your feet touch the flo.

AS WE TRAVEL

Your body is just a vessel one day to be laid to rest.

We stress a lot on the afterlife is our journey just a test.

We linger in our own self sorrow not knowing where to turn.

As we travel in life's vicious cycle we forget the lessons learned.

We cover up our transgressions as if He can't see.

Our lives unravel as we travel our road to Calvary.

We stress a lot on the afterlife is our journey just a test.

Your body is just a vessel one day to be laid to rest.

We congregate in awe of you we praise your holy name.

As we deviate from the road you paved your love remains the same.

Mistakes are just a part of life although sometimes we gamble.

Then you step in and show us just enough for us to handle.

So granted we do have choices and our lives sometimes unravel.

You need to take heed those demons will feed choose well the road you travel.

GUN FIGHT

This gun shit isn't new gun violence been around since roads were made of dust.

Before money had pictures of dead presidents and read in God we trust.

Fighting has always been a way of life kings would battle kings.

Now we blame Guns for the senseless killings and the sorrow that it brings.

True Guns are used in violent crimes against both Black and White.

But there usually used by punks and bitches who are just afraid to fight.

Growing up we use to knuckle up and may the best man win.

Man up is the way you handle things to live to fight again.

But somewhere along the line someone lost to many fights.

Ran and came back with a loaded gun muzzle flashes through the night.

Afraid to take an ass whooping a punk run to the gun.

Now that punk ass mentality He has is passed down to his son.

When you don't have any other choice and the numbers aren't in your favor.

Your families at risk calculate all of this then use a Gun to ease the labor.

But punks and bitches are making it hard to legally own a gun.

The ones afraid of physical contact the ones that brake and run.

A new generation of violence is born and we need to make I right.

It's not guns that's killing this generation it's the punks who just can't fight.

ASS WHOOPING

Punishment today no allowance no computer time out.

Punishment when I was a kid ASS WHOOPING!

The government and state legislators or D.C.F.S have made it hard to raise a kid.

When I was growing up and I fucked up I got an ass whooping for what I did.

A belt to ass is not child abuse there is proof this method works.

Here's a list I comprised to contradict the jerks.

Depriving a child of food- CHILD ABUSE!

Locking a child in a closet-CHILD ABUSE!

Beating a child until they bleed-CHILD ABUSE!

Using food money for drugs-CHILD ABUSE!

Leaving a child at home alone for days-CHILD ABUSE!

NOW!

Whooping a child's ass for giving away the last of the food to his friends getting hi. LEARNING EXPERIENCE!

Whooping a child's ass for ditching school. LEARNING EXPERIENCE!

Whooping a child's ass for being disrespectful to elders. LEARNING EXPERIENCE!

Whooping a child's ass for not defending themselves. LEARNING EXPERIENCE!

Whooping a child's ass for being a bully. LEARNING EXPERIENCE!

As one should notice by now the pros outweigh the cons.

I could keep on writing bout ass whooping's cause the list goes on and on.

Sometimes you have to go back to old teachings when children go astray.

What an apple does for a doctor an "ASS WHOPPING" could do today.

We can't discipline or own children when they misbehave.

But an "ASS WHOPPING" is what master used to discipline his slaves.

I know this is a little drastic but I have to plead my case.

A good ole fashion "ASS WHOPPING" a technic that's going to waste.

You want to see change in your children then show them who got the juice.

Just be sure you understand the difference between Ass Whooping and Child Abuse.

YOUNG KILLINGS

I watch the news on tv each day I feel the pain.

My heart is always heavy my eyes begin to rain.

A generation dying, families crying, it's all because of them.

Young killings are becoming all too common life expectancy is slim.

His works are being stolen by the ones that He created.

Parents lives are being crushed young dreams have all but faded.

Young killings all around the world death by Gun Fist and Sticks.

Kids are killing kids and doing it just for kicks.

Programs are being taken away so the streets are where they go.

We're stuck in this haze of madness; the death rate continues to grow.

A change is surly needed of what I have no clue.

I'm afraid young killings will continue no matter what we do.

We can't control the future from mistakes made in the past.

Young killings have become a way of life and the young is dying fast.

Still searching for an answer a relief from all the drama.

When all else fails oh what the hell lets blame it on Obama.

Our eyes have been shut for far too long only Christ can start the healing.

We need to get involved in the lives of our young and pray that He ends young killings.

YOUR ALL HERO'S

IF no one has acknowledged that we came close to losing our lives.

My Vietnam vets that I've spoken to told me don't be surprised.

The country's not calling us baby killers or looking at us with disgrace.

It's not the American people but the government that's slapping us in the face.

Some of us are being treated as if getting hurt was something wrong.

The only true acknowledgment that we received was in a country and western song.

If you had surgery to replace a limb or removed scrap metal from your toe.

Just as those who have died your all heroes in my eyes since the government won't tell you so.

Some soldiers have legitimate injuries and should've gotten a purple heart.

But awards and metals can't ease the pain or replace a missing part.

To my brothers and sister who haven't received the respect or recognition that is due.

I'm proud to be a part of your history I'm proud to have served with you.

YOUR ALL HEROS

THE UNPREPARED

I understand supporting the soldiers fighting in this war.

What I can't understand as an American is what were we supporting bush for?

He played a game with young people's lives and elders just the same.

People well over 50 fighting in Iraqi to me was just a shame.

Being involved in the training of these troops being thrust into a war.

Basic trainings not enough for what insurgents have in store.

I saw soldiers huddle in bunkers you could smell the fear.

Hear them mumbling under their breath why am I even here.

I trained as an infantry soldier it's always been with me.

Some of these soldiers with limited training this is not where they should be.

For weeks they sent instructors in giving classes on basic skills.

I was nervous about the things they were teaching scared is how I feel.

I knew then what we were challenged with at that point I to grew scared.

My fear became my training tool we all were the unprepared.

WHEN ALL ELSE FAILS

You have no need for him when all is going well.

Then it's Jesus! Jesus! Jesus! Out our mouths when all else fails.

When everything is going well you have no desire to please.

Until your forced to live life on life terms now you're on your knees.

The only time your hands come together is when you want to clap.

Now you're screaming please Father please hands together on your knees it's called a reality slap.

For our sins Jesus died in His hands they hammered nails.

Still the only time you can call on Him is when all else fails.

You would think He deserves more of our time if just to say thank you Father.

If the tables were turned would lessons be learned if He said I don't want to be bothered.

Still he helps to ease those burdens be the wind to hoist your sails.

But praise Him very chance you get don't wait till all else fails.

AN AMERICA TERRORIST

We faced our worst terrorist and He was right here in our mist.

He's killed our children at an alarming rate this American Terrorist.

He created a war inside His head then when His plan began to malfunction.

He invented a reason to continue the war called it weapons of mass destruction.

We looked for this cache of weapons which was really never found.

An American terrorist our Commander and Chief really tore this country down.

He was successfully killing a generation at a most alarming rate.

A terrorist walked amongst us in charge of this country's fate.

He walked freely through our airports He had a private plane.

We paid Him to run this country and the man was clearly insane.

He talked about our safety and how much we lived at risk.

He's an American terrorist the one who started this.

We had a terrorist here at home contemplating which button to push.
We were in the midst of an American Terrorist His name GEORGE W BUSH.

THE WAR AT HOME

Drugs flow freely through our streets and our freedom is at risk.

How many more must be sacrificed before we put an end to this.

We went overseas to get Saddam cause He's messing up Iraq.

But we can't defeat the war at home in the form of heroin and rocks.

We have children and Veterans homeless living out on the street.

They have no clothes on their back no food in their bellies and no shoes on their feet.

The government is covering up contracts to keep contractors overseas.

Parents are crying citizens are dying Lord stop this madness please.

Their spending millions of taxpayer dollars to destroy the ozone layer.

Slowly destroying the economy, a generation slayer.

The war at home is escalating were losing parents to the streets.

The war at home is killing futures were heading for defeat.

UNESSASARY ROUGHNESS

They say life is what you make of it still we forget from which it came.

With all the sacrifices our ancestors made we honor them with shame.

Today we look the other way at all this craziness.

In our elders eyes I see the tears they cry due to unnecessary roughness.

We're finding was to eliminate what they fought so hard to get.

If they were here today, I believe they would say, I don't believe this shit.

Senseless killing of our young their existence is at risk.

Can you image a world with no killing what would come of this?

Worlds divided minds undecided our ancestors shake their fist.

We violate the trust of those who died for us unnecessary roughness.

We stand on the shoulders of many we live because they died.

We walk theses streets freely because of the tears they cried.

Beaten and disrespected for civil rights now in the place of this.

We thank them with black on black killings unnecessary roughness.

A vicious cycle of anarchy displayed by the way we live.

They gave their lives for freedom with nothing else to give.

We must understand the past in order to understand the future.

We must bind as a unit as one no color, no language, all religions our ancestors deserve to rest we must stop unnecessary roughness.

TRENCHES AND BENCHES

The time has come again to go out and cast a vote.

Government is so corrupt these days we have no an antidote.

Elected officials are getting rich soldiers are steady dying.

War is killing a generation without even trying.

Still elected officials are safely living with their ass's glue to benches.

Soldiers are dying every day in mud and blood filled trenches.

Gas prices are going down death is on the rise.

The worlds still holding nuclear weapons were trying to act surprised.

The war on terrorism still remains peace is being sought.

Children are being raised in racist homes were hatred is taught.

When Bush was coach of the Government and His cabinet was warming the benches.

Soldiers were dodging bullets and rockets faced down in dusty trenches.

My heart goes out to the families who's loved ones have been lost

When you go out this year to cast your vote remember a what cost.

ABOUT LOSING

With a generation intent on focusing on which joy stick should I be using.

More focus should be on the task at hand worried about losing.

Losing the right to live freely losing the right to choose.

Not paying attention to what's going on in the world smoking blunts and drinking booze.

Babies having babies another childhood is lost.

Giving up the one thing in your life the you control your virginity at what cost.

Then when an adult try to give you advise you show your anger by refusing.

It's about how many cuss words come out your mouth it all about losing.

Losing control of your future trying to raise a child on your own.

Where's the guy who told you he loved you just to get you alone.

Now with a "DEADBEAT" father in your child's life this must be so confusing.

Now you have to protect this child from pedophiles see it's all about losing.

So don't give up something so precious to someone bent solely on using.

Sex to get pleasure violating your treasure remember it's all about losing.

WHEN THEY STRUGGLE

We have no idea of what they're going through and it's not our job to judge.

If you push a child to hard in life usually they won't budge.

A child can absorb so much pain then holds it all inside.

Losing a parent at an early age is like part of you up and died.

They wind up in horrible places and it's hard for them to cope.

Some will never see wealth some stay by themselves some lose the fight to dope.

When they struggle it's an image of me the reflection of a battered man.

Their joys their pains, their losses their gains, their lives are in our hands.

When I see the faces of our children, my troubles seem so small.

Their standing tall in a situation where most adults would fall.

When they struggle we struggle they mimic what we do.

My ancestors gave me the knowledge I needed now I'm passing life's ball to you.

INSIDE A DREAM

Dreams are a part of reality or things we wish we had.

Nightmares are just dreams of agony or thoughts of things gone bad.

We sleep to rest the body we dream to cleanse the soul.

When you're inside a dream it's a warning of stories left untold.

We dream of things we want to achieve or things we think we lost.

When we mimic the things inside a dream does that make them true or false?

Inside a dream we see some things in life we will regret.

Sometimes our dreams are past actions we're trying to forget.

Inside a dream we wash away the things that cause us pain.

But when we awake it's obvious that what ails us still remains.

We can't control this cycle and hard as this may seem.

We live the life we see in our sleep we live inside a dream.

We fall in love inside a dream and wish that it was real.

Then hope when you awaken that person loves you still.

We live inside our loneliness we need a light or beam.

To show us the way to happiness when were inside a dream.

OWNER OF A LONELY HEART

Call it what you want to but relationships are hard.

The more you seem to put into one the further you drift apart.

Never stop treating her with "LOVE AND RESPECT" the way you did at the start.

That's the first step to not becoming the owner of a lonely heart.

Don't stop telling here I love you or giving flowers for nothing at all.

Continue to tell her she's beautiful and be there when she calls.

Now please don't get this twisted she also plays a part.

Cause she can just as easily become the owner of a lonely heart.

A relationship is an equal love that's shared between the two.

It has a negative and a positive side it's like a witch's brew.

Get out of this equation quick take heed to the word behoove.

Hanging around this relationship is a bad career move.

Communication is the key to keeping love alive.

If talking can't pull your nose up your heading for a dive.

Help heal one another's loneliness and end it at the start.

Do and the two of you won't be owners of a lonely heart.

JUST CAN'T STAY AWAY

My emotions are all jumbled up inside I think of you every day.

Loving you has become an addiction I just can't stay away.

I think of you when I'm awake see you when I'm sleep.

Then I awake and realize the truth, then I start to weep.

I know our feelings aren't the same and the price I may have to pay.

Every time I see you these feelings return I just can't stay away.

Sometimes I stare out into space I leave the place I'm in.

My thoughts are of you; I don't know what to do that's when the hurt begins.

I cover up theses emotions with tears no one can see.

But this tears are mere expressions I'm hiding them from me.

My heart has become this clump of steel solid and cold as ice,

I hate to gamble and loving you is just like shooting dice.

I've failed in every relationship leading up to this day.

But ours is not a relationship it's a ship sailing toward relations and I just can't stay away.

THANK YOU FATHER

Thank you Father for giving me life, with you there is no end.

Thank you Father for unselfishly giving your Son to cover all our sins.

Thank you Father for allowing me to live, for watching over me.

Thank you Father cause without you who knows where I would be.

Thank you Father for being my all and all while allowing me to be.

A part of the world in which you created, and the road you paved for me.

Thank you Father for listening to me when, I thought no one else would.

Thank you Father for being my Savior when, I felt misunderstood.

Thank you Father for punishing me for the wrong in life I did.

Thank you Father for reminding me when my head would get to big.

Today I thank you Father for all that you have done.

I thank you for your sacrifice, I thank you for your Son.

DO IT REALLY MAKE A DIFFERENCE?

Republican or democrat what difference does it make?

To error is only human so a chance is what we take.

Does it really make a difference when we go out to cast our votes? They swear to make a difference and find an antidote.

To the current problems that we face be it war or border patrol.

What are we electing these people for they never reach their goal?

They say we're going to make a change and lie to get your votes.

Then get into office and screw things up then find a scapegoat.

To vote is like playing Russian roulette take a chance on the spin.

You never know where the truth ends and where the lies begin.

Does it really make a difference, something always seems to go wrong?

We vote to put them in office then hear the same old song.

So does it really make a difference when we go out on election day?

Just as a baby will cry politicians will lie, just to get their way.

So what difference does it make?

THE TRANSGRESSIONS OF DEPRESSION

The ups and downs of life is like a slow funeral procession.

You live you die you laugh you cry the transgressions of depression.

Is It physical or emotional when one is feeling down?

Will depression be a part of everyday life lived above ground?

If my parents suffered from depression does that mean I will as well?

I'm already facing emotional scars from war, I guess only time will tell.

I tried drugs for my depression when your high you just don't care.

But when the high is over and you become sober the problems will still be there.

Depression is a transgression a part of life we all must face.

You can't run from reality you'll wind up with a case.

We understand that problems are a part of depression, but just like the body needs clothes.

God created problems to keep His children on their toes.

Don't self-medicate your depression it will only prolong your troubles.

Let your knees touch the ground, when you're feeling down don't let the devil bursts your bubble.

See everything in life has a cycle, it moves at its own progression.

Don't give in to sin, look out for false grins, it's all the transgressions of depression.

ENGULFED

Lost within one's inner being like a wild animal I feel trapped.

Engulfed inside a container of loneliness, the lid has just been tapped.

Tightly closed are my emotions as I battle the demons within.

Wrapped tight are my emotions as depression started to settle in.

I tremble at the mere thought of living life alone.

Huddled around my entity that I now call my own.

I settle back into my tormented state I pause to take a look.

Trapped without companionship my life's an open book.

I run to the phone to answer it hoping it would be you.

Set in a fixated dream state not knowing what to do.

I mimic the lives of others wanting what's theirs to be mine.

Holding on to this unhappiness I'll stand the test of time.

Still I grow weary of the path I'm on am I prepared for such a fight.

I'm engulfed in an eternal darkness as I struggle to see the light.

ENGULFED.

COLOR CODED

Segregated by race are we all crayons in a color coded package called earth.

Some people have been programed to not like others hatred taught since birth.

Now it's being called terrorism since were all being hated the same.

As when whites were targeting blacks to be slaves the ugliness still remains.

They say terrorism isn't prejudice I find that hard to believe.

Realizing the two are truly an entity is not that hard to perceive.

ISIL don't like Americans; they don't care about the color of your skin.

Black White Dark Light they just want life as we know it to end.

Our soldiers are dying overseas trying to clean up foreign streets.

Here our children are dying, parents are crying, and our economy is facing defeat. Today it's plain to see that the world we know is corroded. There's no black or white no day no night soon the world well be color coded.

IN HIS HANDS

To worry is in our nature it's a part of our emotional package.

He said give me your burdens, I well relieve your emotional baggage.

There will come a time in your lives, when man has done all He can.

Prayer is the key just believe in thee, put your burdens in my hand

To hurt is only human and fear is a part of life.

You must understand, God has a plan for the husband and the wife. Let His love consume you in your time of need.

A little faith is all you need the size of a mustard seed.

It will comfort you in theses trying times, heal you when you're down.

In his hands you'll find peace of mind and your feet on solid ground.

My prayers will be with you though it be hard to understand.

To worry is in our nature but our lives are in His hands.

I FEEL A DRAFT

When I first heard Bush say forty thousand more troops to Iraq at first it made me laugh.

Then this cold chill came over me I believe I feel a draft.

No one is volunteering anymore and their sending the same soldiers again.

Bush can't foresee a victory or convince us this will end.

On the news we see our soldiers dodging bullets in the streets.

What they don't show is the bodies of our loved ones covered with bloody sheets.

At home we mourn their passing our flags fly at half-staff.

It's coming can't you feel it I tell you I feel a draft.

I'm thinking about joining the Army come on talk to me Dad.

Every time I see that commercial it reminds me things are bad.

Telling the parents to go on line while children are over there dying.

Someone in the white house is smoking drugs I tell you their brains are frying.

We're fighting two wars already our forces are cut in half.

The President is setting the stage for this I tell you I feel a draft.

Troops are leaving in battle gear to fight insurgents in Iraq.

And returning home on cargo planes in a silver unmarked box.

Brace yourself its coming older vets know what's in store.

They're going to start drafting our children to supply bodies for this war.

You think what you see on tv is bad and what you here is scary.

Wait till they till you, you have to go it's no longer voluntary.

WASTED TEARS

Waste tears or waterfalls of pain felt from deep within.

We release these tears of loneliness when the pain begins.

We sink into this hell hole as the tears run down your face.

You can't understand the emptiness you can't recognize the place.

You try to control your emotion confusing as this may seem.

You're trapped inside a nightmare you thought was just a dream.

Crying about something you can't control the beginning of all your fears.

Striving for what's right, you cry out in the night yet still there wasted tears.

The rain cascades down your face you don't know what to do.

The wasted tears from years and years are slowly killing you.

Now given all that you have done and all the tears you've tasted.

With your head held down, no answers on the ground you now see the tears you've wasted.

FRAME'S

Life is like a board game it never stays the same.

A slide show since the day you were born passing by in frame's.

You can't control this cycle vicious sometimes it is.

At times life can be happy at times it brings on tears.

Each day is a new beginning will this agony ever stop.

Will it spin until your world is blurred or until your bottom drops?

Click click each frame brings on change from the days you lived before.

Each frame is a new reminder of what the next day has in store.

You try to rewind in the back of your mind yet the frame's still remains the same.

You struggle to compete every night in your sleep but this madness you can't tame.

Fast forward thru another day while you can still remember your name.

Can't change the frame's click, click, still the same snap the picture and play the game.

WHAT DO WE DO NOW?

After flying to a foreign country, to fight a war for reasons unknown. We return home broken pains in every bone.

My emotions are all bundled up and I can't erase the scenes.

Some Vets return home to become the unknown then wind up a dope fiend.

They poke and prod us as if we were rats to determine if were fit.

To be paid for the pains and sufferings of war that they call benefits.

They run us through training like cattle then send us to Iraq.

Then we return that's when we learn you too will be lost in the cracks.

Now diagnosed with P.T.S.D and given drugs by the pound.

They try to charge you for the drugs how the hell does that sound.

What do we do now I ask myself I've lost my job and Wife?

I've lost a lot in defense of this country now I just want a life.

INCARCERATED (AKA) LOCKED -UP

Somewhere in life you made a mistake in lemans terms fucked up.

That's why these bars now surround you and your currently locked up.

Given all that you have done and how this came to be.

Bars have way of bringing your ass back to reality.

Now you must be careful all the time and always watch your back.

Or wind up being someone's bitch! Or married to a guy name Jack.

Hearing newbies crying out at night turnkey help me please!

Next day He's braiding another man's hair with sores on both His knees.

Now your bowels flow freely and your draws are saturated.

Your thinking I could still be anal retentive if I wasn't incarcerated.

Now your pants are sagging off your ass your walking with a switch.

That's the indication that you're the new prison Bitch.

Now you screaming and hollering every night I hear this happens often.

You done gave up your man hood to a big black inmate that the block calls Big Beef Boston.

Your writing letters home to your girl giving her the I'm a Man pitch.

But the last time I visit I couldn't help noticing you walking with a switch. So man up to the shit you did screaming I'm innocent is so overrated.

Admit you fucked up that's why your locked up in lemans terms, incarcerated.

IN CONSTANT ANGER

My blood pressure raises as the teardrops fill my eyes.

In constant anger my body quivers this rage so deep inside.

Constant memories of the war cloud my chain of thought.

Freedom from these tormenting dreams is really all I sought.

Clinging to this sadness I fight to find relief.

Drugs are just a quick fix to help me with the grief.

Cold sweats and agony my bodies riddle with pain.

I sleep to escape the madness to awaken to it again.

I try to fit in a society that I feel has let me down.

Sometimes I pray let this be the last day, my feet will touch the ground.

Dying isn't the answer living isn't the cure.

Every breath I take I contemplate; I'm going to die for sure.

My life is like that winter coat dangling on a hanger.

Every day I live in fear, I live in constant danger.

CATCH A FALLING STAR

Like a diamond starts out as a lump of coal waiting for its day to shine.

A child is destined to blossoms we must recognize the signs.

Lying dormant inside this amazing gift are accomplishments waiting to grow.

That dim light way out in the distance waiting on its turn to glow.

Just as plants need water to sprout new roots a child needs direction to see.

That the images portrayed on tv and in games is not reality.

Parents are facing more these days and children are losing site.

Of what the true value of life is the difference between wrong and right.

So much time is being wasted and the future is looking bleak.

Children are choosing the wrong direction for the dreams in which they seek.

Only God knows their destiny and we can't control their fate.

Yet we can show guidance and maturity when the pressures of life are great.

We understand the code of standards we need to set the bar.

Be that catcher's mitt they need to catch a falling star.

HELP ME FIND MY WAY

In the darkness I've traveled far too long.

I know now it's hopeless, I can't do life on my own.

My wrong turns have convinced me to give up total control.

Let you pilot this vessel that only stores my soul.

I know you been working me Jesus, I was to blind to see.

All the wrong I was doing you revealed it all to me.

Help me find my way Father lift the veil from my eyes.

Tired of living in darkness being surrounded by lies.

Please mold my life dear Father to your hands I am the clay.

I want to walk with you Father help me find my way.

Give me the strength to move forward steer me as you will.

Battle this army of demons help me up this hill.

I'm working hard to focus I'm living day to day.

I hope you're here beside me to help me find my way.

I'M JUST SAYING

My mind is filled with memories a lot of advice was given.

The choices you make in life will define, the life in which your living.

I'm just saying; I can't understand how one can make mistakes constant.

Mistakes are building blocks not a constant part of life.

If you choose to struggle, then you will if you choose to change you will.

It's not difficult If you're in a room full of grown men and two children are being sold you make a choice.

If you get pregnant by a deadbeat that don't take care of one, why would you lay down and have number two?

I'm just saying; if drugs are controlling your life and you've hit bottom why are you still doing drugs?

I'm just saying; we've been given the greatest gift one could receive and we refuse to except it.

You will have choices in life our ancestors choose to fight for us to be free.

The senseless killings of a generation, children have no clue about the word Sacrifice, the word respect, the word achieve.

Those who see a means to an end still have to battle the streets.

Children killing Children for the dream, the street dream and street dreams usually lead to nightmares.

We must show change to teach change, life's short and getting shorter it's not promised. Tomorrow may not come sleep can be permanent. Be blessed every morning your feet touch the floor.

You will make choices in your life, I'm just saying the choices you make today may be a mistake.

But don't choose not to change tomorrow. I'm just saying!

FOREVER I WILL BE.

Forever will I be enchanted by your loving grace.

Concealed within your beauty I find my happy place.

Forever will I be in debt to you; for giving your son to me.

This life I'm living all my sin's forgiven that day on Calvary.

Forever will I be grateful for all that you have done.

I understand that your gift to man was your only begotten Son.

Forever I will be hopeful and give praise to only you.

Because of you I'm humble to be man, Lord tell me what to do.

Forever I will be open to all that you present.

I will follow the path you've lain, forever be content.

Forever I will continue to grow stronger in your word.

I'll take heed to the lesson then share my confession to all this will be heard.

Forever I will be this soul just living in this vessel.

Waiting for the day I hear the Angels say, welcome to His castle.

ETERNALLY

I watch you like a movie you're always in my dreams.

I've scripted out every episode it never ends it seems.

Your imbedded in my memories I hold you in my sleep.

But knowing you're so far away I awaken, I weep.

If this is what love is built on, then this must truly be.

The time for me to let you know I love you eternally.

I live to say I love you it's clear for me to see.

The gift I asked my Savior for has now been sent to me.

If confessions are supposed to cleanse the soul, then I confess my love to you.

My world revolves around this love and everything you do.

You need to understand this you mean the world to me.

A heart once locked and shielded you now hold the key.

To unlock this once closed and lonely heart your love has set me free.
So know this I'm in all the way love eternally.

FINE LATE HITS NOT GREAT HITS

I heard the commissioner say, players need to adjust and practice technics.

Since the time when there was little to no pads and leather helmets the game has been played fast. This is the nature of the game.

I know the greats have to be appalled, their legacy is being tarnished. By bad calls and fines.

You can't slow down the pace of a game that's defined by speed and rewarded with big contracts.

The only way to slow down the game is play slow players or flag football.

You can't expect men to come out of collage playing at full speed to come to the NFL then start playing PEE WEE ball.

The game is too fast to predict no matter how good your technic is there will be hits.

It's a contact sport you are attempting to turn grown men into children.

They know the dangers of the game, for that reason the owner pay.

Now you what to fine them for the same reason you pay them.

Sir if this is the organization you want to lead it's destined to become the N.F.F.L The National Flag Football League.

Watch some old film you need to love the game to respect the game.

The game of football is a part from all other sports.

I'm not saying don't do what you can to make the game safe.

But you can't predict or adjust on the fly, you can't change a man's game into OH NOT SO HARD!

CHOICE IS CHANGE

I see thoughts from within, thoughts that never end.

Just a never ending chain of thoughts.

I pluck pieces of the images in my dreams.

Yet the outcome remains the same.

I have chosen to remain in a stalemate with life.

Still I flock to wrong I must be depressed or life isn't balanced.

I continue to blame others for my choices, the image in front of me is never me.

Still I see thoughts from within, thoughts that never end.

I have become my own worst enemy I have managed to stifle my emotions.

Turn them off like a faucet; off from the world still inside I cry.

I cry inside for change and as this battle inside wages on outside I'm dying.

I see without seeing talk without talking I react without thinking.

I do things to create change still nothing changes.

I have allowed myself a chance to choose change still my change is a choice.

Am I headed in the wrong direction is my choice a change?

Can I emotionally choose to change is choice a change?

SHE LAID

She laid by the waters as the sun glisten off the curves of her body.

She laid I watched the sun shine and cast a shadow of her it was perfect.

As she breathes my excitement went array I watched as sweat rolled down her she laid.

She rolled as if she knew that side of her was ripe, I stood at awe as she laid.

Oh she laid in the sand next to an old log, her heart beating with the rhythm of the rippling waves.

As the tide rolled in so did she, she laid I saw her she laid.

Silently she laid oh so still without motion she laid.

Never have one seen such uneven yet balanced energy, she loomed of loveliness as she laid.

The beauty of her landscaping as she laid was breathtaking she loomed of it.

I absorbed every ounce of her as she laid heavy on my mind, my dreams were of her my thoughts were of her every part of me wanted her as she laid.

I hurt for her I wondered if She felt the same, I wondered why she laid if she hurt for me.

I saw her she laid oh so still without motion she laid, never have one seen such uneven yet balanced energy, she loomed of loveliness as She Laid.

UNIFIED SOULS

These words are inspired by your love, I'm thankful just to be.

Here to witness your undying love for each other and be part of your family tree.

Your kids are grown and on their own, still your love has stood the test.

Together your one; to never be undone, a union that's truly blessed.

Love has no monetary value and it's not something that you owe.

The more two share this style of love, the longer this love will grow.

So many years and counting you won't find this in no book.

The love and care the knowledge you share by casting just a look.

Grounded by the love you share bonded by the trust.

I can only hope that what you have has been instilled in all of us.

God has truly blessed your union thru Him all blessings flow.

So each year on your anniversary I need you both to know.

Life would be meaningless without you, I'm thankful just to say.

I love you more than you'll ever know, your love has paved a way.

The blueprint of love is written and were watching as it unfolds.

God has not only united you husband and wife, He Unified your Souls.

I'M GOING TO LOVE YOU

As long as I'm walking amongst men, with every breath I take.

My love grows every moment with you, my heart my soul I shake.

You move me from the inside, I'm here because of you.

I'd have nothing without you in my life, believe these words are true.

My emotions are running rapid these feelings I can't explain.

It's because of you that my heart beats again and again.

I wonder I'm I worthy, do I deserve the love you share?

Are you truly the love sent from above, can you say you really care?

I can't control these feelings as hard as I may try.

My eyes are like rivers, cold tears make me shiver, understand for you I cry.

My life is like a desert it's your love that quenches my thirst.

Not having you in my life is close to dying, nothing could be worst.

I live to grant your every wish; I breathe your happiness.

Your alive inside my memories your touch I truly miss.

So look deep inside these words I write and know this to be true.

As long as there's breath inside me, I'm going to love you.

OUR ANCESTORS

The true pioneers our Ancestors, it's because of them we're free.

They gave their lives I can still hear their cries, they died for you and me.

Have we followed in their footsteps, can we say we've paved a way?

Would things still be the way they are if they were here today?

We're destroying a lasting legacy by forgetting the works of some.

Is it true the lyrics that moves the soul we shall overcome?

We've managed to shatter a living dream that carried our people for years.

Still we wonder why the elderly cry, their blood, their sweat, their tears.

Respect has lost its place in life our children are taught to be.

In route to jail or the cemetery a menace to society.

Do school really teach our history are our Ancestors represented?

Because the history taught in schools today would have them all offended.

No knowledge of our people or how hard it was to cope.

It started with the whippings and ended with the rope.

We need to teach our heritage before they can walk the path.

To really understand from which they came, what's within their grasps.

We've been given the greatest gift of all the right to say I'm free.

Are we worthy of this privilege are they proud of what they see?

IN CONTROL

Unable to stay in touch with your emotions, confused on which road to take.

Walking in a world that's dark and lonely, unsure of the choices you make.

Can't believe the life that lies before you, you put you in this place.

Can't control the sadness it's causing madness, its written all over your face.

You look for answers in a bottle find questions in a glass.

You drink until you think it's gone, then it knocks you on your ass!

Blaming everyone but yourself for your failures and life direction.

The problem is you can't you see it's you that pain is your reflection.

Now you live life cold and lonely Ice has become your soul.

Still peace is in reach through his words does He teach believe He's in control.

JESUS PILOT THIS VESSEL

I know I'm not the arch that Noah built, but I'm a vessel just the same. I asked Jesus to pilot this vessel like Noah in your Holy name. Sometimes I lose control of this vessel and may steer it astray. Still I know if I ask this misdirection won't last, you'll take the pain away. Jesus pilot this vessel helps me turn my wrongs to right. I've lived long enough in this darkness, please lead me to the light. If I continue to walk in the path of man this direction will lead me too.

A place where there's no angles, no family, no love, no you.

My body is just a vessel; I'm only passing thru.

You said you'll come back to get me I believe this to be true.

That Jesus pilots this vessel, He's all I need to be.

On the path to walk with angels, see the ones who preceded me. Please steer me right my Brother I ask in our Fathers name. If I don't let you drive, I'm bound to nosedive, this road will remain the same.

THE GOOD STUFF

If you don't understand what the good stuff is, then you haven't been witness to the goodness if the LORD.

Some pray and expect (the old right now) on their time schedule.

The LORD don't work on our schedule.

When they wanted wine the mother of Jesus said unto Him they have no wine.

Jesus said, what have I to do with Thee, Mine hour has not come.

She knew that Jesus could solve the wine problem.

Her faith was strong that's why She said to the servants Whatever He say on to you do it.

Jesus turned water into wine but why? He had already told His mother it is not my time.

He did it because He knew Her faith in Him was strong.

Now how much purer can one get than the Mother of our Lord Jesus Christ plus it's MOM.

See He knows our God is not ignorant you cannot expect good stuff if you don't believe.

Without doubt that He can and will deliver, I'm sure we all have testimonies about the good stuff.

That reminds me of the saying He may not come when you want but He's right on time.

God wants us to celebrate He wants us to laugh and enjoy life.

He just wants it done without sinning.

Jesus was interested in social happenings still it's said Christians are no fun.

Could it be some are too busy judging then sharing the goodness of God?

Gods goodness the good stuff like your feet touching the floor this morning, a prayer being answered, a sinner being saved that's the good stuff.

Be pure of heart without doubts, pray and if you haven't been witness to the goodness of the Lord.

Then your faith meter is a little low.

SPIRITUAL ENERGY AND GROWTH

Spiritual Energy and Growth to be wise in the wisdom of the LORD. The body is only a storage unit it stores the soul.

Within the body our souls starve for spiritual energy and growth.

GODS commandments as written thou shall not steal but you can't steal Gods word.

So I borrowed this analogy from the Rev T.D Jakes when you buy a new car it comes equipped with an owner's manual.

Our souls are the same it needs maintained it needs knowledge it needs to absorb wisdom, or like a car it will Fail you.

We have been given His owner's manual inside this manual you will find what is needed to achieve spiritual energy and growth.

You can't get it from pushups you can't get it from wind sprints, you won't find it in the wall street journal or time magazine.

But you can and will find the path to spiritual energy and growth in GODS manual.

When were born or cognitive skills or ability to learn is like a blank CD waiting to have the word of GOD downloaded to it.

So we put man-made objects in front of them, a toy with flashing lights or a children's book.

But we wait to pass on Gods manual.

We are born with wisdom but there must be growth in wisdom to understand wisdom.

Thru wisdom comes strength, thru strength comes growth, thru growth comes knowledge, thru knowledge comes wisdom.

Energy and growth are spiritual gifts be ye followers of Men even as I also am of Christ but I will have you know that the head of every man is Christ, and the head of every women is of man and the head of Christ is GOD.

Just by reading this my spiritual energy and growth soared through the roof.

Now concerning spiritual gifts, I would not have you ignorant.

Your SPIRITUAL ENERGY AND GROWTH will grow through the knowledge and living of His word.

STOP

STOP it can't be worth dying for.

STOP before life as you know it becomes no more.

The Holy Spirit is battling the devil for our souls.

Like man will be battling drug dealers out to steal your goals.

You allowed yourself to get addicted knowing where it would lead. I smoke so it was a scapegoat to say it all starts with weed.

It started the day you started and will stop the day you stop.

You need to find the answer before your heart just up and pop!

Time wasted in recovery thinking man has what you need.

Christ has already shed blood for you, for you man will never bleed. He said believe that I'm the living GOD and fear what I can do. Be pure at heart when you come to Me, I'll be there for you. No Man nor magician can heal you as complete as the Holy Spirit. You'll know when it is with you you'll feel it know it hear it.

I just took a short to the obvious sent the problem to the top.

He said your problems are curable He told me to tell you to STOP.

GOD'S ANGELS

We all have our beliefs and how we choose to believe.

We have a problem believing it's His will when our young just up and leave.

There's always something else involved like disease drunks and gun's.

Bad Doctors in medicine this is not why he gave us his Son.

He sits high and looks low He has His Angels in place.

Believe He has His Angels living among this race.

I believe He wants us all to live long be happy, grow old.

Here you're just hosting a body cause the Father owns your soul.

Joseph lived passed one hundred we can't make it two twenty-one.

God is the only solution because Man don't have none.

Gods Angels are watching over us our loved ones destined to be.

The one blocking the Devils advances protecting you and me.

WHEN THE PILLOW IS NOT ENOUGH

I've searched high and low for companionship for years it eluded me.

I spent plenty of money for the self-proclaimed honey was too damn blind to see.

I've given to much time to this search, the road has been so rough.

So tell me what's a Man to do when the pillow is not enough.

Life has opened up my eyes on how to fill this slot.

While I search for a special someone to fill this empty spot.

I've looked into the eyes of many it was plain as hell to see.

Their mission their goal their purpose was to get all they could from me.

My goals may be a bit to high my standards hard to reach.

I should step back and evaluate my life, practice what I preach.

Stop beating yourself up for Love, stop making your life so tough.

If you paying your playing you know what I'm saying when the pillow is not enough.

THE BOY IS THE FATHER OF THE MAN

I grew up without a father so as I grew to be a Man.

The streets became my mentor pain made me understand.

The Boy a playful Kid inside trying to understand.

Why the streets are so hard on Him, He has no future plans.

The Boy is the Father of the Man; His teachings are far from true.

So He lives the life on an innocent child not knowing what to do.

He longs to be a Father figure with nothing to compare Himself.

He's the offspring of His Father, Whom He lost to failing health.

The man inside is crying out, the Boy don't have a clue.

Either the streets are going to educate or beat the man out of you.

You're fighting against wisdom stupidity blinds you from the light.

So now your gangbanging and running the streets at all times of night.

He's reaching out to the father who Himself is just a child.

A grown ass man with no life plans unfocused and running wild.

How can He make a commitment, give the Boy the room to grow?

He can't comprehend the world; His knowledge of life is slow.

Now he's fighting within Himself, the Boy can't understand.

So it's up to the Boy to teach the Father how to be a Man.

So remember your never too old to learn grasp it while you can.

Listen to your inner child as the Boy become the Father of the Man.

I'M NOT RACIST

I'M NOT RACIST! I could care less about what color you are.

It shouldn't be Called racist it should be called STUPID!

Anyone who judges you because of the color of your skin is just that.

I'M NOT RACIST! It's not the color of your skin I don't like 'it's you.

Your attitude your demeanor, your personality isn't something I really want to deal with.

I'M NOT RACIST! I can deal with anyone on any level stupidity is not a race it's a group.

A group of people who believe they are superior to everybody.

You're not Racist your STUPID.

We must understand that racism is not genetic this evil is taught.

I'M NOT RACIST! so if you're doing stupid and your teeth leave your gums it's not because I'm Racist. "YOUR STUPID".

DEADLY DAYS VIOLENT NIGHTS

Close your eyes for a minute now tell me what you see.

Darkness has engulfed the world not just your community.

St louis Chicago, Afghanistan, Iraq.

The death toils are rising as if it were a stock.

It doesn't matter when it doesn't matter where.

Deadly days Violent nights you can feel it in the air.

Death has become the weapon used for Greed' Lust' and Religion.

Glamorizing the deaths of policemen, Children being taken by unqualified, untrained, unlicensed, unbelievably stupid Parents.

Rock throwing Diss slanging store looting criminals have become the new way to protest.

During the early part of the day they emerge be it a Gangbanger, Drug addict Disgruntle employee a Soldier with P.T.S.D.

Lives have been taken families are shaken, baby's bodies being found in lakes.

Race is being used as a platform, to mask the fact that people are just killing people.

As the light turns to darkness the Devils horns emerge.

The night becomes a death zone as though were in a purge.

Bullets ring out through the night bodies line the streets.

A child alone and dying on the hard cold concrete.

Sirens screaming through the night a chill howling through the wind.

You awake to the of an empty space that howling was a friend.

Black lives matter White lives matter; Police lives matter all lives matter.

VIOLENT DAYS" VIOLENT NIGHTS" Blacks and whites doesn't matter when or where you can feel it in the air.

WHEN I WRITE

Locked inside my mind words and phrase tend to fight.

They congregate like an angry mob unstable when I write.

Strong thoughts and emotions form images in my mind.

As if the ink has consumed the blood in my veins then on paper they seem to find.

A place to express the anger the heartache, the pain.

When I write I free the person that without writing would go insane.

A lifetime jumbled up in words crying to get out.

Silent echoes in my mind I dream, I wake, I shout.

My thoughts are sometimes cloudy dark and sort of dense.

Yet when I write the words bring comfort, does that make any sense?

I write about the loves I've had about the loves I've lost.

Without these words to guide me the end comes with a cost.

My poetry lives within me it's like my second site.

It shows me the true meaning of life so clearly when I write.

WHAT DO I DO NOW?

The draft had nothing to do with it, I'm proud of what I've done.

I'm sadden by the fact that the war has not been won.

P.T.S.D has changed my life; I can't hold down job.

I feel helpless since returning, I feel like I've been robbed.

Of the ability to inner act with others, feel safe again at home.

My life is in a bubble I live inside a dome.

Sometimes I just can't understand the what, the when, the how.

Afraid I've been forgotten so what do I do now?

Iraq has changed the way I live with the medicines I take.

Has caused me to isolate when I'm alone I tremble, I shake.

My health is not what it used to be I jump when I hear POW!

I don't want those returning to go through this, so what do I do now?

Trying to adapt to life because what I thought I knew has changed.

The fighting goes on in my mind the terrains been rearranged.

I want to live a normal life after war I don't know how.

Not giving in to life's roads of sin but what do I do now.

IN HIM

I've always felt His presence in my dreams I see his face.

In Him I found my purpose, I crave His Holy Grace.

Because of Him I have the life I have, He gave me a choice.

I pray to Him in my time of need, I know He hears my voice.

I live my life accordingly I try not to go astray.

Giving Him the praise that He deserves, that's how I start my day.

I need His word to guide me, I need His words to cope.

I chose to believe there is a He just to have some hope.

A little faith is all you need there will always be wrong and right.

Get down on your knees pray please Father please, before you lay down at night.

Your burdens will be lifted just take the time to say.

I give my burdens to you LORD please make them go away.

With Him I know I can make it even when times are grim.

GOD put us here for a purpose why not believe in HIM.

THROUGH IT OIL

How long did we truly think it would take before Nukes entered the game?

The death toll has only gotten higher since the capture of Saddam Hussain.

Do you remember Operation Desert Storm when we supposedly conquered Iran?

Now they have just as many guns as us bought from AMERICANS.

Right dab in the middle our Soldiers sat while Bush was giving warnings.

Between Iraq and Iran, we took our stand praying to be there in the morning.

Bush had our military stretched so thin He wanted to bring back the draft.

He put Troops your children in harm's way were going to feel their wrath.

These Countries over the decades has stocked up on the weapons needed.

Train an army of radicals of the parents we defeated.

See hate isn't genetic it's taught so why are we trying to be their police.

Trying to instill our way of life on them we know not their idea of peace.

The speeches are always centered on hate, children dying on foreign soil.

It wasn't the terrorist we were fighting still we fought through it oil.

IN THE NAME OF LOVE

I love rolling over in the morning, the first thing I see is you.

I'm reminded that love is possible, that our love is true.

Your glow is like a beam of light in search of only me.

Shining brightly around us for all the world to see.

My life would have no purpose, just a meaningless lump of man.

Only you can save me lift me up hold my hand.

My heart is always filled with joy whenever your around.

A beautiful diamond laced in gold in you is what I found.

I need to have you always I can't survive a day.

Without telling you I love you, will never go away.

He sent me what I needed a gift sent from above.

He gave me what I needed in the name of love.

WAR STORIES

War stories an addict's worst nightmare or strongest tool.

Can either help to lead you back to life or return you back to fool.

You can't control these stories the pain reflects your use.

The vicious cycle your living in is now called drug abuse.

We share them in our meetings in attempt to find some peace.

An over load of pressure waiting to be released.

A reminder to the addict of the life they held so dear.

We may jubilate at this pleasure yet we live in constant fear.

Of returning to the stories back to where we been.

A vicious cycle these WAR STORIES, will the madness ever end?

Some glorify their war stories tell them with a since of pride.

When the only thing that should be glorified is the fact that you haven't died.

War stories should be used in your recovery only as you deem fit.

War stories your stories my stories the same boat load of shit.

NO DOUBTS ABOUT LOVE

Living my life, the best way I can, knowing it would be a struggle if you were my man.

The feelings I have are so true and so deep, they couldn't reach the everlasting mountains I wander in my sleep.

If the feeling isn't mutual it wouldn't faze me, because the feeling I have inside would last an eternity.

I see you and I together for a life time, knowing that whatever happens you will always be mine.

In my heart your one of my best friends, know this for you my love will never end.

We say we love each other anytime we feel the need.

But I need to know through our troubled times will our love succeed?

Just by me looking at you brings a smile to my face.

Just need to let you know nobody will never take your place.

By Venisha McPherson

INNER MUSIC

My heart is the conductor the leader of my inner music.

It plays a melody so sweet it addictive to the soul.

I harmonize my inner music as it flows softly through my veins.

Vibrating ever so gently like strings in a piano flawless.

Each breath is Cora grafted, a simultaneous sigh of beauty.

These colorful notes mixed with lyrics, can send your emotions in a spin.

So smooth and easy this inner music is a feeling with no end.

It sooths me when I'm angry lifts me when I'm down.

I have to create my own because there's nothing good around.

Inner music deep within me out my mind and cross my lips.

Sending waves of energy through my fingertips.

Writing to release it the ink flows dark and quick.

Filling the pages with love anger, pain my INNER MUSIC.

THE COMMON

As I struggle and face the fact that life isn't always what it seems.

To be blunt life is just a chain reaction of bad nightmares and good dreams.

Bound by facing reality yet divided between real and fake.

Still you cover up your pass transgressions with the choices that you make.

You lie to cover up for the bad choices, decisions you've made in your life.

Now you stand alone all your love ones are gone, someone else is loving your wife.

It's not that hard to contemplate life's not always as you see.

You can't control your future or foresee your destiny.

You attempt to correct your short comings while lying to yourself.

The common is draining your life's forces, robbing you of your health.

You can only control the moment you're in, can't predict the hours to come.

Yet that common moment may be all you have, may be the last for some.

Stay true to the dreams your dreaming, through faith they will come true.

Don't let the common trials and tribulations in life take those dreams away from you.

NEVER AGAIN

When you've given all you have to give, there is no giving back.

See you have nothing else to give because you got addicted to crack.

When the smoke cleared it was obvious you made a big mistake.

The friends you thought you had in your corner were all no give just take.

Even those who vowed to be there, never let you down.

Never again depend on a friend who for money stays around.

Nobody likes you when you're broke, my phone would ring off the hook.

Now my phone hardly ever rings it's just a flip open telephone book.

The blame lie's solely on my shoulders, I let this cycle begin.

I have to detach myself from these fake asses so called friend.

See nobody owes me nothing, I never said hey pay me back!

Time to get my life together pull myself up from the cracks.

To say you hate someone to me is committing a cardinal sin.

So I'll swallow my pride, remember the ride, just say never again.

THE CORNERSTONE

This is the beginning of a new legacy, the end to a reoccurring nightmare of hatred self-centeredness and taught racism.

We stand now at a new Cornerstone in History, but at the beginning of a long awaiting dream.

We can now start a new chapter in the book of our ancestors, the names changed but the pain still remains.

The echoes of slavery still linger in the minds of our Elders.

The younger generation is baffled they have no clue of how when or why.

People have changed teachings have not in some parts of the world Blacks are still recognized as Niggers, Coon, Darky.

White Men and Women are still called Honkey Whitey, Europeans.

But this was not genetically passed from generation to generation this madness is taught.

As we stand at the Cornerstone of change the process has to change, the teachings need to be correct, our ancestors deserve to be acknowledged His- story need to be taught as History.

No matter how painful, degrading this may be we all played a part in History.

Still some choose to sit in the darkness of the pass, pass down the hatred that has clouded their minds for decades, not see life as an equal.

Love has no color Love has no monetary value, yet still it is the glue that bonds us.

But we still undermine the phrase Love others as you Love yourself.

Because of this, this is the beginning of a new legacy the beginning of reoccurring nightmares of hatred self-centeredness and taught racism.

We stand at The Cornerstone of History but at the beginning of a long awaited dream.

WHEN I CLOSE MY EYES

I'm at peace when I close my eyes my mind is so at ease.

I have no depressing worries no one I have to please.

I see a world that's not at war a child that's glad to be born.

Parents that love, trust one another not a family torn.

When I close my eyes I seek inner peace that's sometimes hard to find.

When my eyes are open its impossible to live inside my mind.

So I isolate myself, for a brief minute while there it seems.

I went back to when my eyes were closed, I'm back inside a dream.

I hurt when my eyes are open because I don't like what I see.

The world today is suffering with no identity.

When I close my eyes I have no worries my life seems so complete.

It's a shame the only time I can find peace is when I go to sleep.

Our lives are filled with chaos poverty, war and lies.

I can only see peace and happiness when I close my eyes.

SHE'S AMAZING

She's the strongest Women I've ever known, I'm here today to say.

I'm here because of the genetic code found in Her D.N.A.

She raised me through my childhood groomed me right to be.

The man that stands before you for all the world to see.

People turned their nose up at the children she as rising.

Alone she raised her family I swear she's so amazing.

She never ran from struggles, she faced them proud and strong.

She's amazing in my eye's; she could never do no wrong.

Her eyes were always filled with hope no matter how hard the times.

She fought through all adversities was always in Her prime.

Times weren't always happy; times weren't always sad.

I never knew my father She was my Mom and Dad.

MERE WORDS would be hard to describe Her, She's gone, I'm still praising.

The fact that She's my Mother, that She's So Amazing.

YOU LIED TO ME

You said you'll always love me our love would never end.

Once our love completed me now the pains begins.

Loneliness engulfs me only you can set me free.

Without you I'm so empty a minutes an eternity.

You told me this was endless, I thought this love was true.

The more you shared your love with me the more my passions grew.

I gave you my everything my heart for you to hold.

You vanquished loves integrity brought weakness to my soul.

You carefully maneuvered your will on me like a vulture I was your prey.

Though the scars run deep within me I still can't stay away.

Your poker face was flawless it was hard for me to see.

You played me DAMN! YOU PLAYED ME! Oh well you lied to me.

HER

Her smile is like a beacon brightly shining for all the world to see.

Her scent is like a breath of fresh air that softly awakens me.

Her kiss is as soft as a rose pedal so gentle to the touch.

Her body shaped like an hour glass oh I love so much.

Her being has become a part of me that, I choose not to share.

Her color is peanut butter from her feet up to her hair.

Her big brown eyes excite me to the point of no return.

Her name is echoed inside my heart her love is all I yearn.

To her I'm just a mystery a book she hasn't read.

To her I'm a blur a memory resting in her head.

I dream about her when I'm sleep want her when I'm awake.

I crave her touch every morning with every breath I take.

I can't control my feelings I just can't stay away.

I need her she completes me in your name dear Lord I pray.

THEY DIDN'T ASK TO BE HERE

Our children are dying to often too soon, living in a world of fear.

They may cry out for attention but they didn't ask to be here.

Babies are having babies why their still babies at heart.

They have no clue of what to do, don't know where to start.

They can't control their emotions their hormones are running wild.

How gloomy this world must look when seen through the eyes of a child.

This vicious cycle their living in the future is so unclear.

Being abused for being born but they didn't ask to be here.

They know nothing about their history or how they came to be.

Free to choose your future to build a dynasty.

The streets are raising children; it's becoming plain to see.

Their lives are going nowhere it's up to you and me.

To brake this vicious cycle let me make this perfectly clear.

Where the reason this generation is failing they didn't ask to be here.

A HEART ONLY GOES WHERE IT WANTS

If your ever in a relationship, your partner decides to cheat.

A heart only goes where it wants to which leads between the sheets.

If you have to fight to prove your love you should stop and evaluate.

The infrastructure of your relationship maybe the struggles just too great.

The heart has its own navigation system it knows just what to do.

Clearly now it's obvious a heart goes where it wants to.

It zeros in on its prey like an eagle to a fish.

Sometimes it lies in dormant waiting to grant your wish.

It will weave through your emotions like a needle through a quilt.

Then drop you like a wet blanket, leave you full of guilt.

The heart only goes where it wants to its easy for the mind to say NEXT!

Real easy for the mind to go astray when it's a choice between love or sex.

Commitment doesn't mean confinement when love comes straight from the heart.

Trying to compete for affection is like a halfway erection or not putting the horse before the cart.

If I need is all you hear after you both have shown affection.

The heart only goes where it what's to in this case the wrong direction.

The heart is an emotional muscle beating flawlessly in your chest.

The heart only goes where it wants to it never has to confess.

EMOTIONALY YOURS

The mere thought of you excites me, loving you is so easy to do.

Where ever I go you're with me Lady, I'm so in to you.

Your smile brightens the darkest of times lifts me up when I feel down.

I prayed for someone like you, a true love I have found.

The strengths I find within your eyes push me toward perfection.

With that my love I have no problem showing you my affections.

My loop was incomplete, with you I'm where I need to be.

My ends are now meeting because you complete me.

You're the reason I breathe air each day, it's because of you I live.

God blessed me by creating you to Him my all I give.

I write these words for only you, my love doesn't rain it pours.

I love you more then I love myself, I am emotionally yours.

You've given me so much of you, it's hard for me to compete.

The first time I laid eyes on you, I stumbled to my seat.

Your beauty mesmerized me your will is beyond compare.

There's a glow that engulfs your inner being people stop and stare.

In awe at all that you are oh you mean so much to me.

Today and for always with you I want to be.

So I write these words for only you, my love doesn't rain it pours.

Together Forever for Always Emotionally Yours.

YOU MAKE ME FEEL THIS WAY

I can't explain this feeling it's with me every day.

It only happens when your near me, you make me feel this way.

My thoughts are always of you you're like a summers breeze.

My legs become like Jell-O you bring me to my knees.

The thought of you engulfs me, you're the reason why I say.

I love you, I need you, you make me feel this way.

I sigh when I'm around you as if I need to sleep.

I'm sad when you're not near me, sometime I want to weep.

It's hard to control these feelings for some guidance I do pray.

Lord let this be the one for me you make me feel this way.

NOT JUST TODAY

I found myself searching for the right words to say.

The love and respect I have for you not just today.

I carry you always in my heart you make me feel this way.

As long as you will have me, I'll never go away.

Say you'll always love me; I'll say the same to you.

I believe He created this union we are a chosen few.

My luck in life began to change the day I saw your face.

I knew then God had made possible for us to share time and space.

My dreams are always of you, I'm glad that you chose me.

To be the man you dreamed of, root to our family tree.

I can't explain in MERE WORDS; just how much you mean to me.

Together we make a beautiful sound we have a chemistry.

So today I see fit for me to admit, that you're the reason I feel this way.

I'll love you till the day the Lord takes me away not just today.

IF ONLY FOR ONE NIGHT

I've written many versions of this, guess I'm trying to get it right.

Believe me when I say I'll be happy if only for one night.

I know we only recently met but I'm blinded by the sight.

Your beauty consumes the universe just constant rays of light.

I cherish all that we have done, I pray with all my might.

That you would let me hold you if only for one night.

I close my eyes and think of you, my darkness turns to light.

Please tell me that you love me if only for one night.

So If this be the last time that were together, then let me hold you tight.

I'll cherish the time you allow me if only for one night.

HOLDING YOU

As the doors to my heart swing open, where I only allow a few.

I opened my eyes to another surprise I wasn't holding you.

Sometimes the darkness clouds my judgement, you adjust my eyes to light. When the picture come clear you're not really here it's my pillow I'm holding tight.

I hold on to these feelings as if it were my life, the memories of these feelings reminds me of my wife.

I can't explain the agony my heart hurts to the core, every time my heart would beat I'd squeeze my pillow more.

I held it oh so closely it was at that point I knew; no object or women could take the place of physically holding you.

TO HURT IS HEALING

I know your hurting now my friend, your pains will go away.

To hurt is healing and oh! What a feeling when you here you'll be ok.

Embrace the feelings to hurt is healing, if you wake up and feel no pain. Scream until you here the beep! Then go back to sleep wake up, try it again.

That hurt you feel is normal it will only help you heal. The tears you shed proves you're not dead, will improve the way you feel. So go ahead let it go remember to hurt is healing.

The process may be slow and hard but love will see you through.

Keep Christ in your life faith in your heart, and love in all you do.

I know your hurting now my friend the pains will go away. To hurt is healing I know the feeling gets better day by day.

FIND MYSELF IN YOU

For years I was lost in loneliness not knowing what to do. Then you walked into my life, I could find myself in you.

I prayed someday to find you, like a miracle there you were. I fell to my knees screaming please Father please let this be Her.

The day you came into my life made my life complete. It was meant for me to find you; it was destiny we meet. The more time we spent together I knew this to be true. I was lost until I met you, I find myself in you.

I TO HAVE A DREAM

Dr. King had a dream I to have a dream, I to have a dream that someday drugs gangs, guns will no longer consume are children's way of life.

I to have a dream that our children's, children will again understand the value of life, stop killing each other with no emotion or resentment.

I to have a dream that babies will stop having babies, so the choice of abortion won't even hit the table.

I to have a dream that books, school supplies will again fill our children's book bags, not knives, guns, and our schools will again become the safe havens they once were.

I to have a dream that racism will stop being taught, we're not born with hate in our hearts it's introduced by man it is not genetic.

I to have a dream to once again see our parks filled with laughing children playing, not grown-ups drinking drugging, using the park as a day time club.

I to have a dream that mothers will stop feeding their unborn child drugs, that in the long run affects society, because of an unwanted addiction they may be the ones to shatter the dream.

I to have a dream that child abuse and abandonment will end, men will stop beating women and vice versa, families will be just that a Family.

I to have a dream that war will be no more, countries will police themselves, young soldiers from all countries will stop dying parents will stop crying, and peace will enter into the hearts of all people regardless of race or religion or sex.

I to have a dream That the dream will be taught in some context in schools. I to have a dream that our future will be in the hands of those who understand the why and how, their able to say the words I'M FREE!

I to have a dream that a cure for all ailments will be found by our future generations, people will live long lives death will not be introduced to our children's children while their still children, the words natural causes will in the cause box nothing else.

I to have a dream; Kings dream Malcom's dream, Rosa's dream, our ancestors dream. I to have a dream that our dreams don't become nightmare's, reoccurring slaps in the face of our ancestors, brought on by a generation that dropped the ball that our ancestors carried in order for us to be here.

Dr. King had a dream; I to have a dream that someday, SOMEDAY! We all will understand "THE DREAM" see our future through Kings eyes, through Malcom's eyes, through our ancestor's eyes through our children's eyes, "I TO HAVE A DREAM".

GUESS YOU DIDN'T KNOW

Trying to put the right words in play to describe them, would likely land me in jail.

But to say they lie cheat and steal is the way to begin this tale.

They lie in their commercials they lie in every speech.

They tell us what they think we want to hear, knowing it's out of reach.

They rob us of our money to keep their bank accounts on full.

Then tell us the deficits still in red, now that's a bunch of bull.

With election time upon us the truth will now come out.

All the dirt you did while in that office is what all the talks about.

But guess you didn't know beforehand all the dirt you now know?

All the corruption and lying that was going on, now AWAY WE GO!

All of a sudden you telling the truth about all the wrong they did.

So you can get in that office and wait for the highest bid.

I guess you didn't know about the stealing, didn't know about the lies?

Now for votes you're a tell all book right before our eyes. The most corrupt business in America, we let them choose our fate.

We now have a Nazi spuming hate saying he can make America great.

They run for these offices for their own wealth to grow.

The question we should be asking at the start of every election, I guess you didn't know?

WISH I COULD CALL HEAVEN

I'm always thinking about you I always see your face.

I miss the conversations; the way your food would taste.

I miss you getting angry about the choices that I made.

You taught me to be efficient, make sure your bills are paid.

I wish I could call heaven so you could hear me say.

I love you mother one more time if only for today.

I wish I could call heaven to talk to you Annette.

To say how much, I miss you, the things I now regret.

I wish there was a connection from here to talk to you.

Your gone and I'm so lonely, I don't know what to do.

A private line to heaven to talk to those we lost.

No landline, no wires, and most of all no cost.

I know it would likely start with three and certainly end with seven.

When I need you I always have this thought, I wish I could call
HEAVEN.

WHY ARE WE DYING

Bright eyed and full of life; a child walked up to me crying.

He asked me in a concerning voice Sir! why are we dying?

My eye wells filled with water as I searched for words to say.

I didn't have an answer still I couldn't turn away.

Why are there guns in schools He asked, why do we go to war?

Why on every corner is there a church and cross the street a liquor store?

Why are they taking God out of school, why are excuses flying?

Why can't I find the answers for this child without just straight out lying?

It's hard to face our children seeing the life they have to live.

It's sad we don't have the answers or the right advice to give.

We're showing them everything that's wrong blinding them from what's right.

Their dying and we don't have an answer our children black and white.

I see them, it hurts me inside their souls are crying.

Their screaming out for guidance, want to know why are we dying?

GIRL X

I can't feel nothing but anger and pain for whomever the culprit must be Insane.

A darken hallway a nine-year-old girl what's going on in this crazy world?

I feel this child as I sit here and write, as the tears fill my eyes throughout the night.

I try to find solace I can't understand, what triggered the animal inside this man.

I feel for the parents who are stricken with grief, put your child in God's hands when seeking relief.

I'll pray for you Girl x your forever on my mind come back to your parents you'll heal in time.

Your life is so precious your life is so pure for all the pain in this city Girl x is the cure.

Bring us together show us the light come back to us baby girl, make things right.

To whomever the culprit turn yourself in you've already committed a cardinal sin.

Harming Gods children, no matter what age get your hands on a Bible and read every page.

For Girl x will pull through our prayers run wide you need the LORD in your life from Him you can't hide.

YOU MAKE ME FEEL THIS WAY

I can't explain this feeling but it's with me every day.

It only happens when your near me you make me feel this way.

My thoughts are only of you feels like a summers breeze.

My legs become like Jell-O you bring me to my knees.

Just the thought of you engulfs me you're the reason why I say.

I love you, I need you, you make me feel this way.

I sigh when I'm around you as if I need to sleep.

I'm sad when you're not near me, sometimes I want to weep.

It's hard to control these feelings for guidance I do pray.

Lord let this be the one for me, you make me feel this way.

MOTHERS LOVE

To put these words together was plain as day to me.

You gave me all the love you could, worked your chemistry.

I know it's hard as hell these days to raise a child alone.

Yet you raised me plus two makes three, did this on your own.

I watched you work throughout the years to get the things we need.

My Mother was never a follower my Mother was born to lead.

She struggled through the hardest times, she laughed when She was mad.

Her heart was filled with nothing but love until you made Her mad.

No one could ever replace the love you freely choose to give.

I'll forever cherish and miss her undying love as long as I shall live.

REMEMBER WHEN

Remember when it was safe for children to play outside, parents weren't worried, nobody died?

Remember when parks were filled with children, full of play and filled with life? There were no guns no drugs, no ropes in trees, no knife.

Remember when Officers were friendly, sometimes we knew their names? Respect was given no matter how your living, we all were treated the same.

Remember when disciplining your child was not called child abuse? Gangs weren't killing kids to get what we call back then juice.

Remember when ending your day on the porch was part of your daily routine? Now seating on your porch could wind up being a murder scene.

Remember when neighbors knew each other, from one end of the block to the other? Now they don't even speak though they pass every week, don't even acknowledge one another.

Remember when life had value it was just worth living, remember when it wasn't about how much you're getting but more about what your giving?

Remember when our elders would talk to us, drill it until we get it? Today their afraid to speak to the young, afraid of becoming a statistic.

Remember when remembering when was worth remembering when? Now what will their kids remember when they start remembering when?

WHERE DID WE GO WRONG?

How did we get to where we are now, what started this downward spin?

Was it the crack generation or the heroin, or just according to the skin I'm in?

People are killing people as if it were a sport. young men are spending time in jail for not paying child support.

We have people strapping bombs to their bodies, killing children women and man.

Believing the lie that when you die you'll enter the promise land.

Were outraged by the violence; its killing off a race, the proof is acknowledged by the anguish and pain seen on our elder's face.

The tears they cry are ours, they cry for what they see, all the drugs and killings in our community.

This vicious cycle we live in has haunted us for too long, I fear the end is near so where did we go wrong?

BREAKING BAD HABITS

A desire or a craving for what is forbidden by God.

I've faced countless battles with cravings and desires.

I've fought and fought, I've tried my way, I tried man's way, still the desires and cravings were still there.

See every bad habit we endure is infused by choice.

God knows all! That's why he gave us the gift of choice.

We know and understand the difference between right and wrong.

Which opens the door to bad habits, cause if you choose wrong and continue to do wrong it becomes HABIT!

But I (say that again I) made the choice to do them.

Now there are bad habits that we chose to call bad, like smoking cigarettes, grinding your teeth, sucking your thumb, bad habits.

These will not hinder your entrance into Heaven. But the ones that will hinder your entrance are referred to in the Bible as CONCUPISCENCES.

Which means desires or cravings forbidden by GOD, lying cheating, fornication, stealing do the ten commandments ring a bell.

Anyway we can go on and on about evil concupiscence's but what is important is this.

As his children we will all be tempted, we will all have our share of bad habits. But what bad habits will you allow to enter your life?

Can you deal with the consequences that come with that choice?

Now when breaking bad habits, you can get caught up in manmade remedies, be fighting this battle alone with man (GOOD LUCK). I had to remember how I was finally able to break my bad habits. After failing man's way and my way, the only way was GODS way. So let me say this; we have to teach our children to raise their children "CHRIST LIKE".

Teach them about the bad habits that are forbidden by GOD. Because everything that is forbidden will be introduced to them. It's how we prepare them to make the CHRIST CHOICE".

IN WHICH WE LIVE

Born in the Sixties I have knowledge to give.

To clarify the changes to life in which we live.

I didn't have a two parent home, still I turned out pretty well.

Even though I had Elders tell me I'd be a bum, Dead, or in Jail.

I played in parks as a little kid, I didn't always do what's right.

I stole some candy; snuck in the pool, broke curfew some nights.

I cursed in front of my Elders had sex at an early age.

Well I thought I did you know how it is, we all went through that stage.

I Gangbanged growing up trying to fit in, for years I called them Family, Brothers, Friend.

I fought when I was growing up, probably lost more than I won.

But we knuckled up one on one, and no one pulled a gun.

I saw racism in the Military introduced to willing minds.

A racist praying on Soldiers that's where I learned the signs.

I've recovered through Drug Addictions, so there is knowledge I could give.

To clarify the changes to life in which we live.

PRAY FOR MY CITY

Too much killing going on! "PRAY FOR MY CITY"!

How many more will we mourn! "PRAY FOR MY CITY"!

Finding Babies in Lagoons "PRAY FOR MY CITY"!

How many murders before noon "PRAY FOR MY CITY"!

Too much anger on the streets, can't control the outcome.

Too much danger in the streets, Drugs, Gangs, and Guns.

Will we ever see the peace, our Ancestor's died for.

Tell me will the violence cease, what does the future have in Store?

Living life in my City is becoming extinct, looking dark in my City kind a hard to think.

About planting roots in my City, can't raise a family here.

Too much death in my City, were living in fear.

Can't walk the streets in my City, Can't sit at home in peace.

Need you to "PRAY FOR MY CITY", we need a release.

Kids killing Kids in my City, Mothers mourning the lost.

Not educating our children, and this is the cost.

Bullets ring out through the Churches, Cops killing unarmed men.

Gods children are dying and that's a cardinal SIN.

Man can't correct the problem. My City's bound to FAIL!

Man has turned what GOD has given us into a living HELL!

Man's laws are failing the people, my City's afraid of change.

Were stuck in a vicious cycle, and our leaders are Deranged.

I need you to "PRAY FOR MY CITY" in its darkest of days.

We're walking around in a fog, living life in a daze.

I'm crying tears for My City, My City is living in HELL!

Blood stains cover the streets; bodies fill the JAILS!

I hear the screams in My City as it screams in the night.

Please "PRAY FOR MY CITY: BECAUSE IT'S LOSING THIS FIGHT!

I want to thank GOD for blessing me with this gift, without Him there would be no me.

My life has been blessed I have no regrets; I have accomplished a dream.

I'm proud to be able to share this dream and gift with the world.

Thanks to my family and friends who put up with me and my swings.

Thank you to my new friends at "HALO PUBLISHING", I know I was a handful being new at this but you stood by me; I can only hope my book does well for your company.

Enjoy "MERE WORDS" it was an enjoyment to write, I can only hope it's the same to you as you read it.

THANK YOU

CASSIUS DELOARTIC MCPHERSON

Special Dedication
To my sons
Kevin Robinson & Byron Nelson
MY SON'S

I'm not the Dad that made you still I love you just the same.

My Son's became My children when your Mom chose to take my name.

You witnessed all my failures as I struggled with the street.

I hope I showed you how to be strong and never taste defeat.

I watched you grow as children to teenagers then to MEN.

Through time you became more then my children my boys became my FRIEND.

My life in no way was perfect I struggled to find my way.

Still I never stopped loving my children and that STILL rings true today.

Your vessels are no longer with us, this I can't explain.

I know that losing you cause me grief heartache and pain.

But the memories live within me those will never go away.

When I'm feeling down and lonely those memories make my day.

I think about our music and the happiness it brings.

I know MY SON'S are in heaven and the wind beneath my wings.

CPSIA information can be obtained
at www.ICGtesting.com
Printed in the USA
FFOW01n1842090816
26649FF